How Big Is It?

Written by Meg Jones

Illustrated by Teri Gower

"How big is it?" asked Kate.

"This big," said Joe, spreading out his arms.

"Let's find a way of measuring it," Kate said.

Joe went to find Mum.

"How can I measure something?" asked Joe.

"With a ruler," said Mum, as she carried on reading.

Joe looked at the ruler. It had measuring marks all down the side.

He took the ruler into the garden and showed it to Kate.

"We can't use that. It's too short," she told him.

Joe tried again.

"How can I measure something?" he asked Grandma.

"With a tape measure," said Grandma, as she carried on hammering the floor.

Joe picked up the tape measure and showed it to Kate. They stretched it out as far as it would go.

"It's still not long enough," said Kate.

Kate and Joe went into the garden shed to find Grandad.

"How can we measure something?" asked Kate.

"Mmm," mumbled Grandad, looking around. "What about using a metre stick?" he said at last. He pointed to a long piece of wood propped up in the corner.

Kate and Joe took the metre stick outside but it was still not long enough.

"It's no good," said Kate. "We'll never be able to measure it."

Just then, Frazzle the dog came running round the corner. He was carrying a ball of Aunt Jessamy's knitting wool in his mouth. Aunt Jessamy was close behind him.

Kate and Joe liked Aunt Jessamy. She was always good fun.

She jumped in front of Frazzle and stopped him in his tracks. He dropped the wool. He looked very pleased with himself as he wagged his tail.

Aunt Jessamy chuckled. "You rascal!" she smiled, patting Frazzle on the head.

Then she saw Joe and Kate standing by her side.

"What are you two doing here?" she asked.

"We are trying to measure this," they said, "but it's too big for us."

"What about measuring it with my ball of wool?" she said. Aunt Jessamy always had an answer for everything.

Joe and Kate had never heard of measuring things with a ball of wool. They thought about how they could do it.

"I'll bend it down, and you hold the wool against it," Aunt Jessamy said.

Joe held the end and Kate unrolled the ball of wool. When she reached the top, Kate broke off the wool.

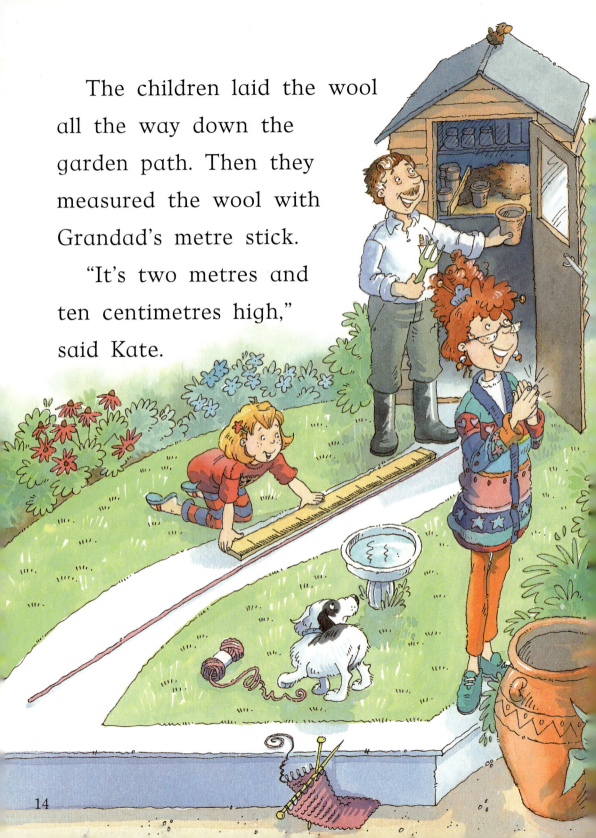

The children laid the wool all the way down the garden path. Then they measured the wool with Grandad's metre stick.

"It's two metres and ten centimetres high," said Kate.

"Wow! Let's celebrate," Joe shouted. "It's the biggest sunflower we have ever grown."

"Congratulations!" everyone cried.

Frazzle got so excited by all the noise that he ran away with Aunt Jessamy's ball of wool.

"Stop!" everyone called to Frazzle. But it was too late. He had wrapped the wool all round Aunt Jessamy!